—*Bible Studies*—

FINDING CONTENTMENT

Carolyn Nystrom

in 6 or 12 studies
for individuals or groups

With Notes for Leaders

INTERVARSITY PRESS
DOWNERS GROVE, ILLINOIS 60515

InterVarsity Press is the book-publishing division of InterVarsity Christian Fellowship, a student movement active on campus at hundreds of universities, colleges and schools of nursing in the United States of America, and a member movement of the International Fellowship of Evangelical Students. For information about local and regional activities, write Public Relations Dept., InterVarsity Christian Fellowship, 6400 Schroeder Rd., P.O. Box 7895, Madison, WI 53707-7895.

All Scripture quotations, unless otherwise indicated, are taken from the HOLY BIBLE, NEW INTERNATIONAL VERSION. Copyright © 1973, 1978, 1984 International Bible Society. Used by permission of Zondervan Publishing House. All rights reserved.

Cover photograph: Robert McKendrick

ISBN 0-8308-1145-1

Printed in the United States of America ∞

15	14	13	12	11	10	9	8	7	6	5	4	3	2
03	02	01	00	99	98	97	96	95	94	93	92		

Contents

Welcome to Christian Character Bible Studies

What is a Christian character? And how does one go about developing it?

As with most questions of faith and the practice of faith, the best source of information is the Bible itself. The Christian Character Bible Studies explore a wide variety of biblical passages that speak of character development.

The Bible speaks of love—love for ourselves, love for God, love for other believers, and love for those who do not yet believe.

The Bible speaks of responsibility—responsibility for the poor, responsibility for the weak, responsibility for the environment, responsibility for our assets, responsibility to work and responsibility to share our faith.

The Bible speaks of holy living—honesty, sexual purity, mental discipline, faithfulness, courage and obedience.

The Bible speaks of hope—a hope that is based on the character of God, the work of Jesus Christ, and an accurate view of our human limitations. It is a hope that says, "Residence on earth is temporary; residence in heaven is eternal."

This series of Bible study guides will help you explore, in

thought and in practice, these many facets of Christian character. But why bother? Why can't we accept ourselves the way we are? Isn't that the route to mental health?

Not entirely. We are all in transition. Each new day brings new influences on who we are. We respond—and change. With God's help, that change can be toward Christian growth.

Growing in character is satisfying. It carries with it the sense of growing in godliness—into the image that God created us to be. It carries a sense of harmony, of walking hand in hand with God. But it is not painless. Therefore these guides will constantly ask us to hold up our character to the mirror of Scripture and to bend that character along the lines of Christ's image. God doesn't want us to stay the same. We should allow the Spirit to nudge us through these studies toward the spiritual maturity that God designed for his people.

What Kind of Guide Is This?

This is an inductive Bible study guide. That means that each study deals with a particular passage of Scripture and attempts to understand its content, its meaning, and its implications for godly living. A variety of questions will explore all three of those areas.

This is a thought-provoking guide. Each question assumes a variety of answers. Many questions do not have "right" answers, particularly questions that aim at meaning or application. Instead, the questions should inspire users to explore the passage in more depth.

This study guide is flexible—you can use it for individual study or in a group. You can vary the amount of time you take for each study, and you have various options for the number of studies you do from the guide. This is possible because every guide in this series is structured with two unique features. First, each of the six studies is divided into two parts, and second, several questions are marked with an asterisk (*), indicating that they may be

Guidelines for Using the Christian Character Bible Studies				
Option	Type of Use	Time Allowed	Number of Sessions	Your Plan to Follow
1	Individual	30 minutes	12	Divide each study into two sessions, and use all the questions.
2	Individual	45 minutes	6	Use one study per session, and skip questions with an asterisk (*) if time doesn't allow for them.
3	Individual	60 minutes	6	Use one study per session, and use all the questions.
4	Group	30 minutes	12	Divide each study into two sessions, and skip questions with an asterisk(*) if time doesn't allow for them.
5	Group	45-60 minutes	12	Divide each study into two sessions, and use all the questions.
6	Group	60 minutes	6	Use one study per session, and skip questions with an asterisk (*) if time doesn't allow for them.
7	Group	90 minutes	6	Use one study per session, and use all the questions.

skipped if time does not allow for them. So you can have six sessions or twelve, with varying amounts of time to fit your needs.

How do you decide which approach is best for you? Looking at the chart on page 6, decide if you will be using this guide for individual study or in a group. Then determine how much time you want to spend on each session and how many sessions you want to have. Then follow the plan described in the far right column.

For example, if you are using this guide in a group, you can choose from options 4, 5, 6 or 7. If you have 45-60 minutes for study and discussion in each group meeting, then you can use option 5. Or if you have only 30 minutes available, you can use option 4. These options allow you to have twelve meetings by breaking at the dividing point in each session and using all the questions, including those with an asterisk.

If your group has only six meeting times available, then follow the column headed "Number of Sessions" down to options 6 and 7. Option 6 provides for 60-minute sessions without the asterisked questions while option 6 allows for 90-minute sessions using all the questions.

Note that there are four plans that allow for in-depth study— options 1, 3, 5 and 7. These use each of the questions and will allow for the most thorough examination of Scripture and of ourselves.

With seven different options available to you, Christian Character Bible Studies offer maximum flexibility to suit your schedule and needs.

Each study is composed of three sections: an introduction with a question of approach to the topic of the day, questions that invite study of the passage or passages, and leader's notes at the back of the book. The section of questions provides space for writing observations, either in preparation for the study or during the course of the discussion. This space can form a permanent record of your thoughts and spiritual progress.

Suggestions for Individual Study

1. Read the introduction. Consider the opening question, and make notes about your responses to it.

2. Pray, asking God to speak to you from his Word about this particular topic.

3. Read the passage in a modern translation of the Bible, marking phrases that seem important. Note in the margin any questions that come to your mind as you read.

4. Use the questions from the study guide to more thoroughly examine the passage. (Questions are phrased from the New International Version of the Bible.) Note your findings in the space provided. After you have made your own notes, read the corresponding leader's notes in the back of the book for further insights. (You can ignore the comments about moderating the dynamics of a discussion group.) Consult the bibliography for further information.

5. Re-read the entire passage, making further notes about its general principles and about the personal use you intend to make of them.

6. Pray. Speak to God about insights you have gained into his character—and your own. Tell him of any desires you have for specific growth. Ask his help as you attempt to live out the principles described in that passage.

Suggestions for Group Study

Joining a Bible study group can be a great avenue to spiritual growth. Here are a few guidelines that will help you as you participate in the studies in this guide.

1. These are inductive Bible studies. That means that you will discuss a particular passage of Scripture—in-depth. Only rarely should you refer to other portions of the Bible, and then only at the request of the leader. Of course, the Bible is internally consistent, and other good forms of study draw on that consistency, but inductive Bible study sticks with a single passage and works on it in-depth.

2. These are discussion studies. Questions in this guide aim at helping a group discuss together a passage of Scripture in order to understand its content, meaning and implications. Most people are either natural talkers or natural listeners. Yet this type of study works best if people participate more or less evenly. Try to curb any natural tendency to either excessive talking or excessive quiet. You and the rest of the group will benefit.

3. Most questions in this guide invite a variety of answers. If you disagree with someone else's comment, say so (kindly). Then explain your own point-of-view from the passage before you.

4. Be willing to lead a discussion. Much of the preparation for leading has already been accomplished in the writing of this guide. If you have observed someone else direct the discussion two or three times, you are probably ready to lead.

5. Respect the privacy of others in your group. Many people speak of things within the context of a Bible study/prayer group, that they do not want as public knowledge. Assume that personal information spoken within the group setting is private, unless you are specifically told otherwise. And don't talk about it elsewhere.

6. Enjoy your study. Prepare to grow. God bless.

Suggestions for Group Leaders

Specific suggestions to help you appear in the leader's notes at the back of this guide. Read the opening section of the leader's notes carefully, even if you are only leading one group meeting. Then you can go to the section on the particular study you will lead.

Introducing Finding Contentment

Our house is inhabited by three cats. They allow us humans to pay the bills and share their space. In exchange for this privilege, we are required to feed them, brush them, take them regularly to the vet, and open and close the door (on request) dozens of times a day.

My husband and I often admire the lives of our feline creatures. They snooze in the sun, stretch full-length for a purring belly rub, then curl up to snooze again—the picture of contentment. "In my next life," my husband jokes, "I'm coming back as a kitty cat."

But human contentment is more elusive than a nap in the sun. Like all "higher beings" we need the basics—food, shelter, rest. But does that make us content? Rarely. The wealthiest among us will testify that the most elaborate form of these basics does not in itself bring contentment. We are too complex for that.

So what creates contentment, if, in fact, we are ever able to achieve it? Certain intangibles come to mind: trust, love, joy, peace, comfort, hope. Not physical things at all. But attitudes, feelings, states of being.

God knows of these longings we have for the intangible. Scripture is full of descriptions of these longings. As we search its pages and press them to our own lives, we can begin a path to contentment.

Will we ever find cat-like contentment on earth? Only in bits and pieces and glimpses. And maybe that is as it should be. The writer of Ecclesiastes at the close of his exquisite poem about time ("a time to be born and a time to die") strikes a discordant complaint about time, even at its best: "God has also set eternity in the hearts of man."

Even when we have gotten time into a perfect balance, we still aren't content. Why? God has given humanity, beings created in his own image, the goad of eternity. And it is the intangibles, like trust and love and joy and peace and comfort and hope that will prepare us for forever. With him.

Carolyn Nystrom

ONE

TRUST

Exodus 13:17—14:31

*I*t started with Joseph.

The year was about 1700 B.C. Joseph's brothers sold him to Egypt with the hope of getting rid of an uppity brother. But Joseph had risen to power in Egypt, so much so that he had all of the nation's food at his disposal and answered only to Pharaoh. It was an interesting position to be in when his brothers, plagued by famine in their own land, appealed to Egypt for help. And Joseph helped them. He arranged for them to live in the best land in Egypt.

Joseph lived and prospered in Egypt until the ripe old age of 110. But at his death he insisted that his family promise to take his bones back to Canaan, the land where he was born. Perhaps he remembered God's promise to his great-grandfather Abraham that God would send his people into slavery in a strange land, but that some four hundred years later, God would bring them out again and return them to the land he had promised them.

Slavery came. A new string of pharaohs, hostile to the Hebrews, rose to the throne. Honored guests in the land became beaten slaves. But they continued to grow in number. The book of Numbers estimates their count (432 years after Joseph) to be two million strong! Small wonder that the pharaohs feared them.

Of those days the Scripture records that God said, "I have heard [my people] crying out because of their slave drivers, and I am concerned about their suffering." So God called Moses to lead the Hebrews out of Egypt and back to Canaan. When a series of negotiations with Pharaoh failed to win freedom for the Hebrews, God followed with a series of plagues. Then God said, "Pack up and leave." And even Pharaoh agreed.

Part One

1. Think about your last moving day. What kinds of hopes and fears did you have at that point?

Read Exodus 13:17—14:31.

*2. If you were telling this story from the point-of-view of a Hebrew man or woman, what would you say?

*3. Now try telling the story from the point-of-view of an Egyptian observer.

4. If you were a Hebrew in this procession, what variety of influences, cited in this text, would encourage you to leave Egypt (13:17-22)?

5. How might these conditions have affected the ability of the Hebrews to trust God?

6. In practical terms, what reasons did the Egyptians have to be confident, and the Hebrews to be afraid (14:1-12)?

7. What do God's plans for the Egyptians reveal about his nature?

***8.** God twice told Moses, "I will gain glory through Pharaoh and his chariots and his horsemen." How do you reconcile this aspect of God's glory, as it is portrayed here, with his loving, forgiving character?

9. What details show the degree of the Hebrew fears?

10. Do you think it is easier or harder for you to trust God in a time of uncertainty? Why?

***11.** When have you admired someone's trust in God in the face of uncertainty?

*12. When has your own trust in God helped you find contentment in times of uncertainty?

Part Two
*13. Think back over your past and recall one of the more unsettled stages of your life. What difficulties in faith did you encounter at that point?

What did you feel that you needed from God?

What did you learn about God at that time?

Read Exodus 14:13-31.
14. If you were a Hebrew looking back at the Egyptians in hot pursuit, would the words of Moses in 14:13-14 inspire confidence in you? Explain.

15. What did God tell Moses to do?

16. What specifically did God promise?

17. What all did God do?

*18. If you had been Moses standing on the far bank of the Red Sea, what mixture of thoughts and feelings would have crossed your mind when God said the second time, "Stretch out your hand over the sea"?

*19. Exodus 14:31 says that after the exodus experience, "the people feared the LORD and put their trust in him." What could the Hebrews know of God at that point?

What could they not know?

20. What effect did the events of this chapter have on the faith of the people involved?

21. What has God done in your own past that has helped you to trust him?

22. Complete this sentence: "I would like to trust God more fully for. . . ."

*optional question

TWO
LOVE

Ruth

I have a son-in-law. But my daughter, his wife, is dead. It is small wonder that I feel kinship with Naomi in the book of Ruth.

Like Ruth, our son-in-law has treated our family with the greatest consideration since Sheri's death two years ago. But I remember with a pang the first time he introduced me by name, without the added title "my mother-in-law." But how can a young single man have a mother-in-law? And why should every casual introduction include the tragic story that explains that occurrence?

Like Naomi, I too grieve for lost grandmotherhood. Our daughter was pregnant with our first grandchild when a car accident killed her—and the child. The picture of a red-haired baby with his intelligence and her musical talent, wrapped in my hand-stitched quilt, rocked to sleep in our three-generations-old rocking chair, died that same morning. I am bereft of both daughter and progeny.

But like Ruth and Naomi, our family has discovered, in this tree stump of an in-law relationship, a large measure of love. It is not a love of marriage vows. Those no longer apply. It is not a love of family name. That is different too. It is not a love of history. Our total history together is only six-and-a-half years. It is a love of choice.

Will our choice to love carry us through a future marriage or future children? It is too soon to say. But the book of Ruth brings me hope.

Part One
1. When you think of your grandchildren, or future grandchildren, what hopes and plans do you have?

Read Ruth 1.
2. What disasters brought Naomi to the words of verse 20?

3. How did time and geography contribute to the family's hardship?

4. Why might Naomi's words in verses 8-9 have been difficult for her to say?

5. In what ways did Naomi express love for her two daughters-in-law (vv. 6-15)?

6. What cost was Ruth willing to pay for her love for Naomi?

7. What was Naomi's understanding, at this point, of God's work in her life?

8. How would you explain God's role in what happened to Naomi?

*Read Ruth 2.
*9. What can you know, from this account, about the people and customs of Bethlehem?

*10. In what different ways did Ruth show love and consideration for her mother-in-law?

*11. How did Boaz show his care for Ruth?

*12. Study more carefully the words of Boaz in verse 12. What does this reveal about his understanding of God's nature?

*13. When have you felt protected and loved by God?

Part Two
*14. What do you think it means to show respect to someone?

*Read Ruth 3.
*15. In what different ways do you see people showing consideration for each other in this chapter?

*16. Ruth said to Boaz in verse 9, "Spread the corner of your garment over me." In view of his prayer of blessing in 2:12, how might Boaz interpret that request?

*17. What do you think Boaz meant when he said, "This kindness is greater than that which you showed earlier"?

*18. What evidence of godliness do you find in the way Ruth and Boaz handled this situation?

Read Ruth 4:1-12.
19. What steps did Boaz take to make this a fair and public transaction?

20. Why do you think that the kinsman/redeemer first said that he would buy Naomi's land and later said that he would not?

*21. Of what purpose is the mention of characters from Jewish history in verses 11-12? (Hint: take a quick look at Genesis 38.)

Read Ruth 4:13-22.
22. Why do you think the focus of the story shifts to Naomi at this point?

23. Notice the proclamation of the women, "Naomi has a son." What did this mean to each of the people in the story? (Consider Ruth, Boaz, Naomi, the people of Israel.)

24. When the women prayed with Naomi, they described Ruth as "your daughter-in-law who loves you." How did Ruth's love for Naomi contribute to the contentment of each?

25. Picture a scene from your own family that is somewhat less than contented. What can you do in that kind of setting that would nurture a love that could lead to contentment?

*optional question

THREE

JOY

Philippians 1:12-26

*I*n *Surprised by Joy* C. S. Lewis describes his journey toward faith as (at first) a search for joy. This journey took him through a variety of philosophers and literary figures. Sometimes he found a "fluttering sensation in the diaphragm" during country walks or deep mental probings. But then the feeling left—as if pointing the way to something else. But what?

Eventually, he came to see those flutterings as "the mental track left by the passage of Joy—not the wave but the wave's imprint on the sand." Then, at age 31 Lewis became convinced of the existence of God. From there he made the slow journey toward personal redeeming faith in Jesus Christ. At first he thought that God and joy might be altogether separate. He wrote, "For all I knew, the total rejection of what I called Joy might be one of the demands, might be the very first demand, He [God] would make upon me."

Instead, Lewis discovered that Joy and God were connected, though not as directly as he had at first supposed. By the close of his faith journey account, Lewis describes joy as a signpost, an enjoyable signpost, that points to God. He writes in closing,

But what, in conclusion, of Joy? for that, after all, is what the story has mainly been about. To tell you the truth, the subject has lost nearly all interest for me since I became a Christian. . . . When we are lost in the woods the sight of a signpost is a great matter. He who first sees it cries, "Look!" The whole party gathers round and stares. But when we have found the road and are passing signposts every few miles, we shall not stop and stare. They will encourage us and we shall be grateful to the authority that set them up. . . .

Not, of course, that I don't often catch myself stopping to stare at roadside objects of even less importance.[1]

Part One

1. Describe an incident of joy in your life that you believe pointed to God.

Read Philippians 1:12-18.

2. What all gives Paul joy?

3. What circumstances facing Paul might keep some people from feeling joyful?

*4. Paul says that some people have been encouraged to speak the word of God more courageously "because of my chains." Why do you think they were able to do this?

5. People who found Paul's imprisonment an inspiration to talk about Jesus seemed to do so for a variety of motives. How would you describe these differing motives (vv. 15-17)?

6. Why do you think Paul did not complain about those who preached out of selfish ambition (v. 18)?

*7. When have you felt irritated with someone who spoke the right gospel but for wrong reasons or with wrong methods?

*8. How do you think you ought to respond to these kinds of messengers?

9. When have you seen someone come to faith in Jesus—even though the "messenger" was less than ideal?

*10. What does Paul's joy in this setting suggest about his view of God's work in his life?

11. Name a Christian whose joy you admire. How has that person's joy in Christ influenced your own life?

Part Two
12. On a scale of one to ten (ten is high), what number would you give your general ability to experience and express joy? Explain.

Do you think you should feel guilty if you are not joyful? Why, or why not?

Read Philippians 1:18-26.
13. Even though Paul is in prison, he speaks of deliverance. What do you think he means by that?

14. Paul says in verse 20 that he hopes to have sufficient courage. Do you find his words of verses 21-26 courageous? Explain.

15. What reasons did Paul give for wanting to live?

for wanting to die?

*16. How do Paul's motives for wanting to live (or die) compare with your own?

17. Study carefully Paul's words of verse 21. What do these words mean on an emotional level?

What do they mean in practical terms?

*18. What ingredients of contentment do you find in these words?

19. Why do you think Paul surrounds this discussion of death with so many references to joy?

20. Note again each of Paul's references to joy or rejoicing in Philippians 1:12-26. How is Paul's joy, as expressed here, different

from a forced smile that denies real problems?

21. If you were to search for Paul's contented kind of joy, where would this passage encourage you to look?

*optional question

---

[1]C. S. Lewis, *Surprised by Joy* [New York: Harcourt, Brace and World, 1955], pp. 106, 219, 230, 238.

FOUR

PEACE

1 Peter 3:8-12; Isaiah 11:1-9

My friend Linden Cole, reflecting on his pacifist Quaker background, tells this story of his experience on a New York subway: "I was riding home from work. The subway was crowded. I was hanging onto a strap near the door. So was a black man in work clothes. So also was a large white man who was very drunk. It was the mid-seventies. Racial tension formed its usual backdrop for any interpersonal action in New York City.

"The white man, so drunk he was barely able to stand, began shouting obscenities at the black man. He called him filthy racial names. He called his mother filthy racial names. He doubled his fist and begged the black man to come at him and fight. The black man turned his eyes away from his assailant. The white man raised the tempo of his verbal barrage. The subway continued to pierce its way under the streets. I clung to my strap and wished for a huge extension of the three-foot space that separated me from the two.

"Meanwhile, something I didn't expect began to occur among the nearby passengers, who were mostly black. A low murmuring of voices, barely audible, aimed at the black man. 'Cool it, man.' 'Easy, take it easy.' 'Cool, brother, cool.'

"In the end, it was a non-incident," says Linden. "Nothing happened. I got off at the next stop. So did the drunk man; he stumbled away into the crowd. Nobody got hit. Nobody slammed a drunk body into mine. Nobody started a race riot. Nobody went to jail. Nobody went to the hospital. But a carload of black people made peace that day. And everybody won."

Part One

1. When have you seen someone create peace?

Read 1 Peter 3:8-12.

2. What qualities and actions does Peter say lead to harmonious relationships (vv. 8-9)?

3. Select one of these qualities and explain how it can lead to peace.

4. Verse 8 speaks of sympathy, love, compassion and humility. Why is sympathy and compassion easier to receive if they come from a person who is loving and humble?

5. What do the terms "called" and "inherit" (v. 9) suggest about

reasons for living in the peaceful way described here?

6. What obstacles would you have to overcome in yourself if you were to return evil or insult with a blessing?

*7. What form could "blessing" take in that situation?

8. In verses 10-12, Peter quotes a section of Psalm 34. According to these verses, what can we do to create peace?

9. In view of verse 12, how can you expect your relationship with God to be affected by your response to these commands?

10. Notice the words "seek" and "pursue" in verse 11. What do these words suggest about the nature of peace?

11. Think of an unpeaceful situation or relationship that touches your life. How have you tried to seek and pursue peace?

12. Take one more quick look at this passage to survey various ways of creating harmony. What more might you do to seek and pursue peace in the situation that you noted above?

Part Two
*13. When you try to visualize peace, what is your favorite hope?

Read Isaiah 11:1-9.
*14. If Jewish people saw this passage as a description of Messiah, what kind of person would verses 1-3a lead them to look for?

*15. What does the picture of a live Branch growing out of a tree stump contribute to your appreciation of Jesus?

*16. "Delight" and "fear" are words not often put together. What do you think verse 3 means when it says that this Branch will "delight in the fear of the LORD"?

*17. Look more carefully at verses 3b-5. Why might people who are poor and needy want the kind of judge described here?

18. Why would the kind of judgment described here lead to peace?

19. Read again Isaiah 11:6-9. How does this picture express your own longing for peace?

*20. Notice the actions described in verses 6-9. What do these add to your picture of peace?

*21. Like many Old Testament prophets, Isaiah saw the future as if it were a series of mountain ridges juxtaposed on a single plane. (Jesus was born as a "shoot" out of Jesse's root, but much of the rest of this prophecy will not come about until his return.) How does the picture in these verses, of a time yet to come, give you hope for your own future?

22. "The earth will be full of the knowledge of the LORD," says verse 9, a hint that the earth itself is flawed at present. What examples of disharmony do you see in the natural world?

What lack of peace concerns you among God's human creation?

23. Our longing for the peace of our real home (in heaven) can cause us to seek and pursue and pray for peace here on this flawed earth. Pray for peace by completing this sentence: "Lord, we pray for peace in/between ⸻." (Include personal, local and international situations.)

*optional question

FIVE
COMFORT

2 Corinthians 1:3-11; Job 38:1—40:5; 42:1-6

*I*t was a sultry night with the mercury barely fading from its one-hundred-degree daytime high. The funeral home air conditioner ground vainly against door openings and closings as some seven hundred sweaty relatives and friends filed in, signed the guest book, and stood a few moments with us in front of our daughter's casket.

Their love, their hugs, their tears, their prayers (though remembered in a blur of shock) fortified us through those early days when nothing in all of God's creation made sense.

In such a large crowd, one might expect one or two kooks. We had only one. A young man, barely known to the family, settled down in a chair next to me and, oblivious to the growing line of people behind him, explained in great detail his particular denomination's theology of death. I'm sure he had good intentions. He hoped to comfort me. But my death-numbed mind, operating at only about ten per cent capacity, barely heard his words. I kept wondering how long the person next in line had waited to shake my hand. Eventually, the young man stood up and went in search of other family members. I think he found them all.

By contrast, I sat across the breakfast table one morning some weeks later with JoAnn, a good friend of fifteen years. She too had experienced a daughter's sudden death. We cried together. Haltingly, I phrased my questions about God. I asked: "Doesn't God grant any extra protection to his own people? Why should I pray for the rest of my children if he didn't even keep Sheri from being broadsided by a truck? Doesn't God owe me something for a life of service to him?"

JoAnn's answers were slow, thoughtful, rooted in her own grief—and the comfort she had received. "I don't think God owes us anything," she said. "He is in charge of life, and death. He sees it differently than we do." She continued, "The why questions don't have answers. Not here. Not now. We are better off, I think, to ask who God is. That forces us to concentrate on his character. That is solid. And that brings comfort."

Both people offered comfort. But only one succeeded in giving it. And she pointed to God.

Part One
1. What's hard about trying to comfort someone?

Read 2 Corinthians 1:3-11.
2. What is the significance of each name for God in verse 3?

3. Find as many purposes for suffering and comfort as you can in this passage.

What do these purposes suggest about the way Jesus, Paul and the Corinthians are connected to each other?

*4. Paul says in verse 4, "God . . . comforts us in all our troubles, so that we can comfort those in any trouble with the comfort we ourselves have received from God." What all do you find significant about that statement?

*5. What have people done that brought you genuine comfort?

6. What value did Paul see to his own suffering (vv. 5-7)?

7. How do Christ's sufferings bring increased meaning to the name "God of all comfort"?

8. How can the sufferings of Christ comfort you in your own current troubles?

*9. In verse 7 Paul says that his hope is firm. How can comfort lead to hope?

10. Paul says in verse 10, "On him [God] we have set our hope." Why can he say that?

11. What have you learned about comfort from your own troubles or grief?

*12. How can you share that comfort as a gift from God?

Part Two

*13. If you were writing a letter of complaint to God about your current circumstances, what would you include in it?

14. Some two thousand years prior to Paul's letter to the Corinthians, Job was in deep trouble. Job had lost all of his animals, all of his servants, and his ten children. He also lost his health. So Job demanded an audience with God. He wanted God to explain all of the trouble that had come upon him. Job got his audience—but not the explanation he had expected.

Read Job 38—39.

What strikes you as awesome about God's speech in this passage?

15. What do you think God wanted Job to understand from this

long list of comparisons between Job and himself?

16. Why do you think God answered Job's questions about the reason for his suffering in this way?

17. Why might you find comfort in an acceptance of God's nature as it is described here?

Read Job 40:1-5 and 42:1-6.
18. Do you think that Job's response to God is appropriate? Explain.

19. Imagine yourself in a situation where another Christian needs comfort. In view of your discussion of the Corinthians and Job passages, what cautions would you take so that you would bring help instead of hurt?

20. What would you hope to accomplish as you extend comfort to a hurting person?

*optional question

SIX

HOPE

1 Thessalonians 4:13—5:11

Grey is the color of hope," wrote Irina Ratushinskaya in her book of that title. She came to that conclusion as she studied her own gray uniform worn in the "Small Zone" reserved for political prisoners in a Soviet slave-labor camp. Beginning in 1982, Irina spent four years in this inner enclosure because of her unrelenting campaign for human freedoms for the people of her country. Ten other women "politicals" lived and slaved there with her. Together they continued their efforts for human rights even within the bureaucracy of prison.

Their clothing had become a harsh tool for punishment. The uniform was loose and flowing (and without undergarments) to increase punishment by cold. It also had a plunging neckline (to entertain the guards?). Yet old Russian women *(babushki)* pieced together the smallest scraps of fiber from bandages, mattress ticking, socks, bits of yarn, to form a "trousseau" for women headed to cold isolation punishment cells.

Irina became the beneficiary of this scrap-made clothing when her husband scheduled the two-hour visit he was allowed three times a year. A prison mate, Pani Jadvyga, took one of these garments, which was covered with oil, and made Irina an outfit to wear for the visit. Her friend worked on the fabric for hours with slivers of soap, then soaked it in bleach, then pieced the resulting soft gray mass into a skirt.

The visit never took place. Guards removed Irina's privileges because of a made-up story that she had not worn a kerchief on her head while crossing the prisonyard. Still her friend's effort constructing the skirt in anticipation of her husband's visit turned its soft gray color into a symbol of hope. It remained so throughout their continuing struggle for justice—even within the Small Zone.

Part One
1. What color would you assign to hope? Why?

Read 1 Thessalonians 4:13-18.
2. Paul says in verse 13, "Brothers, we do not want you to be ignorant." What information does he give here that would prevent ignorance?

3. When you read these words about Christ's return, what sights and sounds come to your mind?

What feelings do they create?

4. Why might the picture painted here be difficult to believe?

5. Verse 14 contains the beginning of an early Christian creed: "We believe that Jesus died and rose again." How could that statement of faith help a person believe the rest of the teaching here?

6. Why does death create a sense of hopelessness?

*7. From verses 13 and 18 what seem to be Paul's purposes in this section of the letter?

*8. If you were to be a part of one of the two sets of believers described in this passage, which would you prefer? Why?

9. What parallels can you see between Christian death and sleep?

10. Would you want the events described here to occur today? Why, or why not?

11. Paul says in verse 18 that we are to encourage one another with these words. What in this passage encourages you?

Part Two

*12. Why do you think that some people try to predict the time of the end of the world?

*13. Would you want to know when Christ will return? Why, or why not?

Read 1 Thessalonians 5:1-11.

14. Why might this passage promote fear in some people and hope in others?

15. What differences do you see between the people of darkness and the people of light?

16. Why might the people of darkness prefer that condition?

17. If you were to warn the people of darkness of their danger, what would you want them to know?

18. Paul says that the people of light are to be alert and self-controlled (v. 6) as they wait for the day of the Lord. What does this mean in practical terms?

19. How can we "put on" faith, love and the hope of salvation?

*20. Paul speaks of faith, love and the hope of salvation as armor. Why?

When have you felt protected by these?

21. Study more carefully the words of verse 10, a possible continuation of the creed that began, "We believe that Jesus died and rose again" (1 Thess 4:14). In what ways are the concepts of these two verses basic to the Christian faith?

22. In verse 11, Paul repeats his command to encourage one another. In what current situations do you need encouragement from other believers?

23. How can the picture of the future as it is portrayed here help you feel hopeful in spite of your current circumstances?

*optional question

Leader's Notes

Leading a Bible discussion can be an enjoyable and rewarding experience. But it can also be intimidating—especially if you've never done it before. If this is how you feel, you're in good company. When God asked Moses to lead the Israelites out of Egypt, he replied, "O Lord, please send someone else to do it!" (Ex 4:13). But God's response to all of his servants—including you—is essentially the same: "My grace is sufficient for you" (2 Cor 12:9).

There is another reason you should feel encouraged. Leading a Bible discussion is not difficult if you follow certain guidelines. You don't need to be an expert on the Bible or a trained teacher. The suggestions listed below should enable you to effectively and enjoyably fulfill your role as leader. And remember the discussion leader usually learns the most—so lead and grow!

Preparing for the Study
Group leaders can prepare to lead a group by following much the same pattern outlined for individual study at the beginning of this

guide. Try to begin preparation far enough in advance for the Spirit of God to begin to use the passage in your own life. Then you will have some idea about what group members will experience as they attempt to live out the passage. Advance preparation will also give your mind time to thoughtfully consider the concepts—probably in odd moments when you least expect it.

Study the flow of the questions. Consider the time available. Plan for an appropriate break (if you are using two sessions) and which optional questions you will use. Note this in your study guide so that you will not feel lost in the middle of the discussion. But be ready to make changes "en route" if the pattern of discussion demands it. Pencil near the questions any information from the leader's section that you don't want to forget. This will eliminate clumsy page turns in the middle of the discussion.

And pray. Pray for each person in the group—by name. Ask that God will prepare that person, just as he is preparing you, to confront the truths of this passage of his Word.

During the Study

1. One of the major jobs of the discussion leader is to pace the study. Don't make your job more difficult by beginning late. So keep an eye on the clock. When the agreed time to begin arrives, launch the study.

2. Take appropriate note of the introductory essay, then ask the approach question. Encourage each of the group members to respond to the question. When everyone is involved in discussing the general topic of the day, you are ready to explore the Scripture.

3. Read the passage aloud, or ask others to read aloud—by paragraphs, not verses. Verse-by-verse reading breaks the flow of thought and reduces understanding. And silent reading often makes concentration difficult, especially for people who are distracted by small noises or who are uncomfortable with group silence. So read aloud—by paragraphs.

4. Keep in mind that the leader's job is to help a group to discover together the content, meaning and implications of a passage of Scripture. People should focus on each other and on the Bible—not necessarily on you. Your job is to moderate a discussion, to keep conversation from lagging, to draw in quiet members, and to pace the study. So encourage multiple responses to questions, and encourage people to interact with each other's observations. Volunteer your own answers only in similar proportion to others in the group.

5. Pacing is a major difficulty for inexperienced leaders. Most group participants have set obligations after a scheduled Bible study. You will earn their thanks if you close the study at a predictable time. But to do so you don't want to race ahead and miss details in the early questions; nor do you want to play catch-up at the end: skipping sections people most want to talk about. Try writing in your study guide the time that you hope to finish questions at various points in the study. This will help you keep a steady pace. Note also any optional questions that you can add or subtract, depending on the pace of the study. But be alert to particular needs and interests in the group. Sometimes you should abandon even the best-laid plans in order to tend to these.

6. If possible, spend time talking about personal needs and praying together. Many groups begin or end by speaking of various worries, concerns, reasons for thanksgiving—or just their plans for the week. Groups who pray together often see God at work in ways far beyond their expectations. It's an excellent way to grow in faith.

7. If you have time, do some further reading on small groups and the dynamics of such groups. For a short, but helpful, overview read *Leading Bible Discussions* by James Nyquist and Jack Kuhatschek (InterVarsity Press). Or for a more in-depth discussion read *Small Group Leaders' Handbook* or *Good Things Come in Small Groups*, both of which are edited by Ron Nicholas (InterVarsity Press). For an excellent study of how small groups can contribute to spiritual growth read *Pilgrims*

in Progress by Jim and Carol Plueddemann (Harold Shaw).
The following notes refer to specific studies in the guide:

Study 1. Trust. Exodus 13:17—14:31.
Purpose: To increase our trust in God by looking at his past faithfulness to his people.
Question 1. Involve as many people as possible in discussing this initial question.
Question 2. Let your group work through the story paragraph by paragraph using the perspective of the Hebrews. Consider sights, sounds, plans, motives, fears and the aftermath.
Question 3. Use a similar technique from the Egyptian perspective.
Question 4. Your group should note that the Hebrews had Pharaoh's permission (13:17), that they followed a route from which return would be difficult (13:18), that they took the bones of their patriarch Joseph—an indication that they would not return to Egypt and that they would have some other land in which to bury the bones. In addition, the Hebrews were led by a cloud and a fire—visible evidence of the presence of God. Once the group has pointed out these details in the text, people can discuss what their own responses might have been to each.
Question 5. Let the group examine how each of the four influences cited in question 4 could influence the Hebrews' trust in God.
Questions 7-8. Those who wish to know God only for his love and compassion and tenderness and mercy, will have some difficulty with this story. God's nature is many-faceted. Use this text to take an honest look at it.
Question 9. See 14:10-12.
Question 10. Recalling the events discussed in questions 15 and 16 may help at this point.
Question 12. Not everyone will be able to answer this question. Contentment is illusive; so is trust. But we who listen to what others have to say can learn from those who testify to this expe-

rience. We can "borrow" their resulting faith.

Question 13. If you are using this study for two sessions, use these questions to open the second session.

Questions 15-17. Let your group spot the details of verses 19-28. The group can follow the discussion better if each participant mentions the verse number with each detail. These are factual questions for which direct answers appear in the text. Use them to examine the text with quick responses, then use the resulting framework of data to move on to subsequent questions of discussion.

Question 18. Verse 25 reveals that the Egyptians were ready to turn back, but did Moses know that? And even if he did, would the Egyptians have changed their minds in a day or two? Use the question to let group members put themselves in Moses' sandals.

Question 19. Of God's nature as it is revealed in the exodus event, Keil and Delitzsch comment, "From this manifestation of Jehovah's omnipotence, the Israelites were to discern not only the merciful Deliverer, but also the holy Judge of the ungodly, that they might grow in the fear of God, as well as in the faith which they had already shown, when, trusting in the omnipotence of Jehovah, they had gone, as though upon dry land (Heb. xi. 29), between the watery walls which might at any moment have overwhelmed them" (C. F. Keil and F. Delitzsch, *Commentary on the Old Testament*, vol. 1 [Grand Rapids: Eerdmans, 1980], p. 49).

Question 20. Compare the Egyptian "faith statement" of verse 25 with God's goals expressed in verses 4, 8 and 17-18. As for the faith of the Hebrews, see verse 31. It is interesting that in the flow of narrative, the closing statement on the exodus story suggests as the result, "the people feared the LORD and put their trust in him and in Moses his servant."

Question 21. Allow time for several people to recount stories from their own pasts that have led to trust in God. Even people who have no such stories will benefit from hearing those who do.

Question 22. Allow a moment for silent thought here and maybe a jotted note. Then try to gain a brief response from each person present.

Study 2. Love. Ruth.

Purpose: To follow Ruth's example of love within our families.

Question 1. Grandchildren may seem far away to any who do not yet have children. But some healthy imagination will enable them to respond anyway. A dash of humor won't hurt.

If your group includes people for whom grandchildren seem unlikely ask, "What memories do you have of your grandmother?" or "What hopes do you have for your spiritual children—and their children?"

Question 2. Use these questions to explore the text of this first chapter.

Question 3. Consult a map to discover the distance and terrain over which the journey to and from Moab took place. Notice also the ten years mentioned in verse 4. Were both Ruth and Orpah infertile during that time? Or were they married late in that period? In view of the text, infertility is certainly possible—and a contributing disaster. For background information on the testy relationship between Israel and Moab, see Numbers 22:4—24:25, Deuteronomy 23:3-6, and Judges 3:12-30.

Question 5. Use all of verses 6-15. If you need a follow-up question try, "How do Naomi's words of verses 11-13 highlight her loss?" Your group should notice that even though Naomi loved her daughters-in-law so much that they kissed and wept at parting, she loved them enough to let go. She cared more about their future than her own loneliness.

Question 6. Study the intense commitment of verses 16-17. For a contrasting follow-up question, ask, "Do you fault Orpah for her decision? Explain."

Question 7. Study Naomi's references to God in verses 8-9, 13, 20-21 and discuss the concepts of God that they reflect. ("What is God like, according to Naomi? What is his nature, his character, his purpose?")

If time permits a follow-up question, ask, "In view of Naomi's view of her God, why do you think Ruth chose to accept Jehovah as her own God?"

Question 8. Don't settle for easy answers here. People have struggled with God's role in human suffering for millennia. It is easy to denigrate Naomi's view of God—until we try to form our own explanation for her suffering (and ours).

Question 9. Survey the chapter with this question. For an explanation of Jewish laws regarding poor people in the community, see Deuteronomy 24:19-22.

Question 10. Notice the details of verses 2, 11, 18 and 23.

Question 11. Your group should point out the information in verses 5, 8-9, 12 and 14-16.

Question 13. Many people will need a few moments to think of an answer to this question. Give the group time to think, then be ready with an example from your own experience. If you are dividing this study over two sessions, end session one after this question.

Question 14. If you are dividing this study into two parts, begin the second part with this question. Depending on the makeup of your group, you might also want to try, "If you are married, how did you give (or receive) a proposal of marriage?"

Question 15. See information in verses 1, 7, 10, 14, 15 and 17.

Question 16. *The NIV Study Bible* comments, "There is a play on the words 'wings' of the Lord (2:12) and 'corners' (lit. 'wings') of the garment (here), both signifying protection. Boaz is vividly reminded that he must serve as the Lord's protective wing to watch over Ruth" (Kenneth Barker, gen. ed., *The NIV Study Bible* [Grand Rapids, Mich.: Zondervan, 1985], p. 368).

Question 17. If you need a follow-up question ask, "How was Ruth's action here a kindness to Boaz? To Naomi?" Since Boaz was related to Naomi, offspring between Ruth and Boaz could continue

Naomi's genetic line. On an emotional level, Ruth's union with Boaz would not take Ruth away from Naomi, thus removing her one remaining family member. Instead, Ruth would add Boaz to the family fold.

For background explanation of Ruth's actions, read Deuteronomy 25:5-6 which established the law of levirate. This law, which may seem unfeeling in light of today's ideals of romantic love, was actually a practical protection to widowed women, whereby they could retain both family and property.

While Ruth's situation did not exactly fit the pattern of Deuteronomy 25, Naomi evidently felt that she and Ruth could claim some of the same protection, particularly if a male relative felt kindly toward them. And Boaz did.

Robert L. Hubbard, Jr., writing in *The New International Commentary on the Old Testament*, says,

. . . attempts to align the customs in Ruth precisely with the details of three frequently cited texts (Gen. 38; Lev. 25:25-34; Deut. 25:5-10) are unnecessary and ill-advised. On the contrary, the value of such texts exceeds their simple, procedural details; rather, they are mirrors of Israel's treasured values. With reference to Ruth, they reflect how strongly Israel valued the survival of families through descendants and family ownership of ancestral property. Finally, one must reckon with how complex—indeed extreme—is the situation told in Ruth compared, for example, to that in Gen. 38 or Deut. 25:5-10. These texts presuppose the relative youth of all parties involved, whereas in Ruth the widow, Naomi, is old. No mention is made of Elimelech's brothers as candidates for levirate marriage; presumably they, like he, are also deceased. Thus, a true levirate marriage is impossible. Even were there a surviving brother, such a marriage would be futile since the text implies that Naomi is physically beyond childbearing age (see 1:11-13). Hence, this situation requires stand-ins for both Elimelech and Naomi if they are to have an heir." (Robert L.

Hubbard, Jr., *The Book of Ruth*, New International Commentary on Old Testament [Grand Rapids: Eerdmans, 1988], pp. 50-51)

Question 20. Survey this section of the chapter for details. We can assume that he did not at first realize that a marriage to Ruth was part of the bargain (vv. 5-6). Perhaps he was already married. Maybe he did not want the added responsibility of a wife—and mother-in-law.

Question 21. Of these names from Jewish history, Hubbard in the New International Commentary writes:

Perez was the oldest of twin boys born to Judah under somewhat scandalous circumstances (Gen. 38). Since Judah refused to give Tamar his youngest son as husband, she posed as a prostitute, became pregnant by an unsuspecting customer (Judah himself), and gave birth to Perez and Zerah. Perez's birth was as unusual as his conception (vv. 27-30). As if pushing his twin aside at the last moment, Perez was born first and earned his name (lit. "breach, breaking out") a portent of his clan's later importance. The words "whom Tamar bore to Judah" recall that famous episode in tribal lore. Its mention probably led the ancient audience to compare that story with the line threatened with extinction, one which later became Judah's leading house, and thereby gained herself fame as its founding mother. If fertile, may not the equally creative (ch 3) foreigner, Ruth, also preserve Elimelech's line, and, if that line becomes famous, thereby earn a similar grand destiny? . . . In sum, the crowd wished Boaz and Ruth a destiny of prosperity and prominence akin to those of the famous ancestors Jacob, Rachel, Leah, and Perez." (pp. 261-262)

Question 22. Compare Ruth 1:20 with Ruth 4:14-16. While the book is named after Ruth, it is really Naomi's story. It is she who undergoes the change so highlighted by this beginning and ending description.

Question 25. If you follow the initial sentence of this question with a brief pause, you will allow people in your group time to form a mental image. Then ask that they respond to that particular situation.

Study 3. Joy. Philippians 1:12-26.

Purpose: To acknowledge the joy in our lives as a gift from God that need not be erased by life's circumstances, because it is rooted in our eternal home.

Question 2. Answers appear in almost every verse. Use the question to survey the passage.

Question 3. Find four or five circumstances in the text that might block a feeling of joy. If time permits a follow-up question, ask, "Do you think that you could feel joyful in Paul's setting? Why, or why not?"

Question 5. Were these rival preachers teaching error, or were they teaching the right gospel for the wrong reasons? *The NIV Study Bible* comments, "These preachers are not to be viewed as being heretical. Their message is true, even though their motives are not pure. The gospel has its objectivity and validity apart from those who proclaim it; the message is more than the medium" (p. 1084).

The passage makes no mention of wrong teaching, but only of wrong motive. Since Paul's whole tone of joy is based on the fact that the gospel of Jesus Christ is continuing to spread, it seems safe to assume that even these rival preachers were spreading the true gospel. If false teaching were spreading as a result of their work, Paul's tone (and tactic) would have been altogether different.

If you want a follow-up question, ask, "What did Paul stand to lose from these other preachers?"

Questions 7-9. Use these questions of personal experience to bring the passage into current focus. As the discussion progresses, be sure to note that Paul is not here condoning heresy. Many of today's evangelists work not only from false motives, but also from a wrong gospel. We may tolerate and even rejoice, as Paul does, that God can use inferior motives and methods to his glory. But we should not encourage a contamination of the basic precepts of the faith.

Question 11. If you are dividing this study into two sessions, end after this question.

Question 12. If you are using this study for two sessions, open your second session here. Linger long enough on these orientation questions for each person to gain some idea of what general mindset he or she brings to the passage.

Question 13. Paul might see deliverance as death (v. 20) or more likely deliverance from prison (see v. 25). It is interesting to note that Paul sees either route of escape as "deliverance."

Question 15. Use this question to explore verses 22-26 in detail. Paul expresses several reasons for wanting to live. Your group should name them. Consider also his desire for death.

Question 18. If you need an additional question after discussing question 18, and if your group is accustomed to trusting honest conversation, ask, "Paul says in verse 23, 'I desire to depart and be with Christ which is better by far.' When have you felt a similar urge?"

Questions 20-21. Some of our guilt over a lack of joy may be false guilt. C. S. Lewis saw joy as a mere signpost that pointed to God. Paul's description of joy relates far more to his position in Christ, his pleasure in seeing other people added to God's kingdom, and his confidence of eternity with Jesus than it does to any personal circumstances.

Answers to these questions should relate in some way to the mindset expressed in question 12. If we are to increase our joy, perhaps we ought to look where Paul found it. Help your group to discuss practical ways of conducting this kind of search.

Study 4. Peace. 1 Peter 3:8-12; Isaiah 11:1-9.

Purpose: To seek peace and pursue it—in our relationships and in our world.

Question 1. The slightest occurrence that led to some measure of peace is a worthy example. After all, the account that introduced the study turned out to be a "non-incident."

Question 2. Note virtually every phrase of verses 8-9.

Question 5. Be sure to discuss both terms from verse 9.

Questions 6-7. Linger long enough on these questions to prompt self-examination and thoughtful ideas about appropriate actions in these difficult situations.

Question 8. Find several answers in these three verses.

Question 11. Ask each person to jot a note of response to this question before he or she attempts to answer it. Even if people have not yet attempted to seek and pursue peace, they should jot the name or situation that is unpeaceful. This will help them prepare for question 12.

Question 12. If you are dividing the study in half, discuss the second part, beginning with question 13, at your next meeting.

Question 14. Study verses 1-3 with this question. Your group should notice a variety of details—including the wide range of ways that God's Spirit is expressed in this person.

Question 15. Your group may have several creative responses. Someone will probably note that Jesse was the father of King David, the greatest king in Israel's history. His direct descendants ruled in Judah for four hundred years until the people were exiled into Babylon in 587 B.C. It was widely prophesied that Messiah would be a descendant of David. People hoped Messiah would restore the Hebrew nation to its former power. Yet, by the time of Christ, the Jewish nation was a mere stump tightly held by Rome. Further, it was a spiritual stump, having repeatedly rejected God's moral laws and the prophets who gave them. All of this (and more) is expressed in the stump/branch image.

Question 19. If you need an extra question at this point ask, "What is your favorite image in this picture of peace?"

Question 20. You can prepare for this question by underlining each verb and picturing its significance.

Question 22. Gather several responses from the natural and the human world. Suggest that the group may also want to think of personal disharmony, perhaps between them and someone else. Spend enough time with this question to prepare for the final exercise in prayers for peace.

Question 23. Invite the group to pray and to support each other's prayers for peace by using the pattern in the guide. Each prayer can be a single sentence. Ask that the group share in each sentence by responding in unison, "Lord, hear our prayer." Encourage people to pray more than once and to meditate during the periods of silence. Close the time of prayers for peace with a simple, "In Christ's name, Amen."

Study 5. Comfort. 2 Corinthians 1:3-11; Job 38:1—40:5; 42:1-6.

Purpose: To give and receive comfort as a gift from God.

Question 2. Examine each name for God and reflect on how that name helps define his nature. If you need a follow-up question, ask, "What can you know of God from Paul's description of him?"

Question 3. Paul writes purposes (or cause and effect) throughout this passage. Among them, your group should notice that we receive comfort so that we can comfort (v. 4), just as the sufferings of Christ flow over our lives, so also our comfort overflows (v. 5), Paul was distressed for the Corinthians' salvation and comfort (v. 6), comfort produces patient endurance (v. 6), just as the Corinthians shared in Paul's suffering, so also they shared in his comfort (v. 7).

Use the information gathered to discuss the implied connections. If you prefer, treat the two questions simultaneously. If discussion of question 3 begins to center on verse 4, just ask question 4 and continue the discussion. (Be sure to first note the information in verses 5-7.)

Question 4. This is a profound statement about comfort. It may even hint at the age-old questions about the purpose of suffering. Encourage your group to carefully examine each phrase.

Question 5. We need not have experienced the death of someone close to need comfort. Troubles, losses, disappointments all invite comfort. Help your group to be as personal, practical and specific as possible. Concrete answers here, based on personal experience, will ease later questions of how we may be of help to others.

Question 6. Find several answers in verses 5-7 and discuss their implications.

Question 8. The question assumes that each person copes with current trouble. The study will have more significance if some of these are brought to the surface and held up to the healing power of Christ's own suffering. Take time to reflect on how Christ's suffering comforts you. Be ready to share your increased awareness with the group.

Question 9. If your group has trouble answering this question, try breaking it down into smaller portions. Ask, "Why might patient endurance lead to the hope Paul describes in verse 7?" Or, "Why do you think that Paul connects trouble, comfort, patient endurance and hope?"

Question 10. Review the text for reasons for the conclusion of hope. If you need a more specific question, ask, "Notice Paul's several uses of the term *deliver* in verse 10; what do these convey of his belief in God?" (Your group should notice the past, present and future uses of the term—and Paul's resulting confidence in God and his character.)

Questions 11-12. Draw on previous responses to help your group make comfort as personal and practical as possible. If you are dividing this study over two sessions, end session one with these questions.

Question 13. If you are dividing this study, begin your second session here.

Question 14. Select a capable reader or readers for this rather lengthy passage. You will all benefit if readers have opportunity ahead of time to prepare to read it with the full expression it deserves. Or you can prepare—and read it yourself.

Linger long enough on this question to allow all of your group adequate appreciation of one of the most lofty passages of Scripture.

Question 15. E. S. P. Heavenor writing in *The New Bible Commentary* answers this way:

> The Word came through a fresh vision of God—of the mighty, majestic God behind the marvels of animate and inanimate nature, painstakingly attentive to the unexpected and the insignificant (see especially 38:26, 27, 39; 39:30), towering above human might and wisdom.
>
> The Word in the vision convinced Job that he could trust such a God. It brought home to his heart the realization that providence was a much more involved and painstaking affair than he had imagined it to be. . . .
>
> God did not answer the problem of his mind, but He did answer Job; He healed the wound of his heart and brought quiet resignation flooding back into his heart. This was not a man who was 'cowed' or 'bludgeoned', but a man who was convinced that all was well with the world because the everlasting arms could not fail." (p. 443)

Your group may come to similar conclusions as it discusses this question. If not, after people have expressed their own ideas, read the above comment as an alternative explanation.

Question 16. If your group needs a more specific question, ask, "Why do you think God did not answer Job's questions about the reason for his suffering? Or did he?"

Question 17. If you want a more personal version of this question, ask, "If Job's picture of God became part of your own soul, how might it bring you comfort?"

Question 18. Your group may have a variety of opinions here.

Discuss them respectfully. If people seem troubled by the words "despise" and "repent" of 42:6, Paul Scherer's exposition of that verse in *The Interpreter's Bible* may help:

It is man's reaction to a devastating encounter with "the holy." . . . The finiteness of the creature is crushed at the sudden onset of the Creator's infinity. Life appears at the conjuncture of being and nonbeing; and before the Being who is the source and the all-embracing mover of his own existence, man shrinks into the infinitely small. Thus Job completes his sentence saying, I . . . repent in dust and ashes. Repent of what? Of ethical crimes which he has not committed? Rather, of the monstrous crime of having condemned his Creator. Job does not receive the verdict of acquittal he has longed for, or the public approval which he craved from his 'vindicator.' But he has no longer any need of them. This does not mean at all that he now discovers the certainty of his own innocence. On the contrary, it is because he is certain of God's care for him that he is able to perceive his guilt. As in the Bible generally, his sense of sin arises at the time of his salvation. . . .

His attitude, therefore, is far from being merely negative. He is redeemed from the anguish, not only or mainly of his tortures, but also of his alienation from the God of his youth. And he repents not from moral guilt, but from a reckless display of distrust. God, whom he accused of acting as a drunken foe, has taken upon himself the gracious initiative of revealing himself in all the glory of the Creator and the Ruler of nature. Job will not approach this God "as a prince" (31:37). He will take his place in the cosmos, trusting in God and saying in effect, "Thy will be done." His trust is the result of his immediate communion (vs. 5) and the cause of his repentance (vs. 6), a repentance which means total dedication. (George Arthur Butterick, gen. ed., *The Interpreter's Bible*, 12 vol. [New York and Nashville: Abingdon Press, 1954], pp. 1193-94)

Question 19. Use these questions to form practical cautions in comfort from all of your discussion thus far. If it seems helpful at this point, refer to the introductory paragraphs of this study.

Question 20. While the previous question helps us limit what we can and ought to do as we comfort, this question should help your group explore comfort with a long view. What are its end goals? Hope? Faith? Renewed trust in God? Emotional and spiritual stability? Return to productive living? These long-range goals can and ought to influence the close-up ways that we give and receive comfort.

Study 6. Hope. 1 Thessalonians 4:13—5:11.

Purpose: To find hope in Christ's promised return.

Question 1. This need not prompt a weighty discussion. Three or four responses with a brief explanation will be enough. Be ready with an example of your own as well.

Question 2. Use this question to help the group locate a dozen or more pieces of information in the passage.

Question 4. Allow time for honest thoughtful answers.

Question 5. Discuss the relationship between Christ's death and resurrection, and the promised coming events. Consider God's love, eternal plan, power, the foretold Incarnation—and its fulfillment.

Question 11. Linger long enough on this question to allow each person to make a personal encounter with the hope reflected in these words.

Question 14. If you need more specific questions, ask, "What words and phrases suggest fear?" "What words and phrases invite hope?"

Question 15. Like question 14, this question also looks for information, though from a different perspective. Use both questions to help your group thoroughly examine the passage. If you need a follow up question, ask, "What is the difference between the sleep of verse 6 and the sleep of verse 10?"

Verse 6 refers to the unbelievers of verse 5 who are spiritually sleeping, while verse 10 refers to whether we physically or spiritually live or die with Christ.

Question 17. To break the question into smaller parts, ask, "What would you want them to know about themselves? about Jesus? about the future?"

Question 20. If people need a question of clarification, ask, "What forms of protection do these offer?"

Questions 22-23. Allow time for personal expressions of need, encouragement and hope.

Carolyn Nystrom lives in St. Charles, Illinois, with her husband, Roger, and an assortment of cats and kids and quilts. She has written over 55 Bible study guides and books for adults and children.

For Further Reading

Aharoni, Yohanan, and Michael Avi-Yonah. *The Macmillan Bible Atlas.* New York: Macmillan, 1977.

Alexander, Donald L., ed. *Christian Spirituality: Five Views of Sanctification.* Downers Grove: InterVarsity Press, 1988.

St. Augustine. *City of God.* 7 vols. Loeb Classical Library. Harvard: Harvard University Press.

Bellah, Robert N., et al. *Habits of the Heart.* Berkeley, Calif.: University of California Press, 1985.

Bonhoeffer, Dietrich. *The Cost of Commitment.* New York: Macmillan, 1963.

Bonhoeffer, Dietrich. *Life Together.* San Francisco: Harper and Row, 1976.

Bright, John. *A History of Israel,* 3d ed. Philadelphia: Westminster Press, 1981.

Bunyan, John. *Pilgrim's Progress.* Moody Classics. Chicago, Ill.: Moody Press, 1984.

Buttrick, George Arthur, gen. ed. *The Interpreter's Bible in Twelve Volumes.* New York and Nashville: Abingdon Press, 1954.

Comenius, J. A. *The Labyrinth of the World and the Paradise of the Heart.* Ann Arbor: University of Michigan, 1972.

Douglas, J. D. *The New Bible Dictionary.* Grand Rapids, Mich.: Eerdmans, 1962.

Ferguson, Sinclair B., and David F. Wright, eds. *New Dictionary of Theology.* Downers Grove: InterVarsity Press, 1988.

Friesen, Gary, and Robin Maxson. *Decison Making and the Will of God.* Portland, Ore.: Multnomah, 1985.

Gasque, W. Ward, ed. New International Greek Commentary. Grand Rapids, Mich.: Eerdmans, 1978-.

Godet, Frederick Louis. *Commentary on Romans.* Grand Rapids, Mich.: Kregel, 1977.

Guthrie, D., J. A. Motyer, A. M. Stibbs, D. J. Wiseman. *The New Bible Commentary, Revised.* Grand Rapids, Mich.: Eerdmans, 1970.

Havel, Vaclav. *The Power of the Powerless*. M. E. Sharpe, 1990.

Hodge, Charles. *Romans*. Edinburgh: The Banner of Truth Trust, 1972.

Hodge, Charles. *Systematic Theology*. Grand Rapids, Mich.: Eerdmans, 1981.

Hubbard, Robert L., Jr. *The Book of Ruth*. The New International Commentary on the Old Testament. Grand Rapids, Mich.: Eerdmans, 1988.

Kuhatschek, Jack. *Taking the Guesswork out of Applying the Bible*. Downers Grove, Ill.: InterVarsity Press, 1990.

Keil, C. F., and F. Delitzsch. *Commentary on the Old Testament in Ten Volumes*. Grand Rapids, Mich.: Eerdmans, 1980.

Kierkegaard, Søren. *Fear and Trembling*. Books on Demand UMI.

Lewis, C. S. *The Screwtape Letters*. Rev. ed. New York: Macmillan, 1982.

Lewis, C. S. *Surprised by Joy*. New York: Harcourt, Brace & World, 1955.

Luther, Martin. *Freedom of the Christian*.

Morris, Leon. *The Gospel According to St. Luke*. New Testament Commentaries. Grand Rapids, Mich.: Eerdmans, 1974.

Nicholas, Ron, et al. *Good Things Come in Small Groups*. Downers Grove, Ill.: InterVarsity Press, 1985.

Nicholas, Ron, et al. *Small Group Leaders' Handbook*. Downers Grove, Ill.: InterVarsity Press, 1981.

Nyquist, James, and Jack Kuhatschek. *Leading Bible Discussions*. Downers Grove: InterVarsity Press, 1985.

Nystrom, Carolyn. *Romans: Christianity on Trial*. Wheaton, Ill.: Harold Shaw, 1980.

Nystrom, Carolyn, and Matthew Floding. *Relationships: Face to Face*. Wheaton, Ill.: Harold Shaw, 1986.

Peterson, Eugene. *A Long Obedience in the Same Direction*. Downers Grove, Ill.: InterVarsity Press, 1980.

Plueddemann, Jim and Carol. *Pilgrims in Progress*. Wheaton: Harold Shaw, 1990.

Smith, Blaine. *Knowing God's Will*. Rev. ed. Downers Grove, Ill.: InterVarsity Press, 1991.

Tenney, Merrill C., gen. ed. *The Zondervan Pictoral Encyclopedia of the Bible*. Grand Rapids, Mich.: Zondervan, 1976.

Tyndale New Testament Commentaries. Grand Rapids, Mich.: Eerdmans.

Wesley, John and Charles. *Selected Prayers, Hymns, Journal Notes, Sermons, Letters and Treatises*. New York: Paulist Press, 1981.

White, John. *Magnificent Obsession*. Downers Grove, Ill.: InterVarsity Press, rev. 1990.

Christian Character Bible Studies from InterVarsity Press
in 6 or 12 studies for individuals or groups

Deciding Wisely by Bill Syrios. Making tough decisions is part of life. Through these Bible studies, you'll find out how to pray for God's will, listen to his voice and become a wise person. These principles of godly decision-making will enable you to serve God in the decisions you make. 1148-6.

Finding Contentment by Carolyn Nystrom. The contentment that characterizes the Christian life is found in intangibles—trust, love, joy, comfort and hope. The studies in this guide will introduce you to these keys to complete fulfillment in Christ. 1145-1.

Living in the World by Carolyn Nystrom. How do we glorify God in secular work? How should we spend our money? What kind of political involvement should we have? This guide is designed to help us clarify godly values so that we will not be affected by the warped values of the world. 1144-3.

Loving God by Carolyn Nystrom. Studies on how God loves—and how his gracious and stubborn love provide the foundation for our love for him. As we learn to love God as he loves us, we'll learn how to be more who he wants us to be. 1141-9.

Loving One Another by Carolyn Nystrom. This guide will help you to solve your differences with other Christians, learn to worship together, encourage one another and open up to each other. Discover the bond of love between believers that is a joyful tie! 1142-7.

Loving the World by Carolyn Nystrom. God has created a glorious world. Our responsibility is to help preserve and protect it. From valuing the sanctity of life to sharing your faith to helping the oppressed to protecting the environment, these Bible studies will help you discover your role in God's creation. 1143-5.

Pursuing Holiness by Carolyn Nystrom. Character traits such as honesty, self-control, sexual purity and integrity may seem out of date. Yet, God's will for us is that we live holy lives. Through Christ, we can find the strength we need to live in a way that glorifies God. These studies will help you to pursue the traits of holiness. 1147-8.

Staying Faithful by Andrea Sterk Louthan and Howard Louthan. This study guide is about wholehearted commitment to Christ. We will be motivated not only to persevere in Christ, but also to grow by taking the risks that will allow us to move forward in our Christian lives. Discover the power of faithfulness! 1146-X.